CW01498354

Awakened Words

John Wesley's Wisdom in a Modern Voice

By Jeremy W. Scott

AWAKENED WORDS:
JOHN WESEY'S WISDOM IN A MODERN VOICE
Copyright © 2025 by Jeremy W. Scott and Foundery.dev
Publishing

All rights reserved.

No part of this work may be reproduced or transmitted in any form or by any means, electronic or mechanical, including photocopying and recording, or by any information storage or retrieval system, except as may be expressly permitted by the 1976 Copyright Act or in writing from the author. Requests for permission should be emailed to contact@foundery.dev.

ISBN-13: 979-8-89766-953-0

All scripture quotations are from the New Revised Standard Version Bible, copyright 1989, Division of Christian Education of the National Council of the Churches of Christ in the United States of America. All rights reserved.

All original works by John Wesley (1703-1791) are in the public domain. Wherever possible original editions were used as the basis for translation.

Contents

AWAKENED WORDS

Introduction

John Wesley, an Anglican cleric and theologian of the 18th century, was a key figure in the development of Methodism, a religious movement that emphasized personal holiness and social reform. Wesley's tireless preaching and organizational skills led to the rapid growth of Methodism, which became a major force in British religious life. Wesley was also a social and political reformer, advocating for issues such as education, poverty relief, and the abolition of slavery. His writings reflect his diverse interests and provide a valuable insight into the religious, social, and political landscape of 18th-century Britain.

This collection offers a fresh encounter with the timeless wisdom of John Wesley writings. Wesley's insights into faith, discipleship, and the Christian life remain as profoundly relevant today as they were centuries ago. Yet, the language of his time, while beautiful, has often presented a barrier, obscuring the depth of his message for many modern readers. Until now, a portion of his brilliance has been veiled by the nuances of 18th-century English.

I undertook this project after teaching a class on Wesley's original writings to a group of lifelong Methodists. I found myself frustrated with the fact that so much of our time together was taken up decrypting the arcane language rather than grappling with the important ideas he was trying to convey. When I first introduced versions of the text I had updated into modern English the whole experience shifted for the better.

Thanks to the incredible advancements in AI tools, we can now bridge that linguistic gap with both less effort and increased consistency. This collection presents Wesley's original writings in modernized English, carefully done to retain the technical accuracy and theological precision of his original intent. I celebrate this breakthrough, not as a replacement for Wesley's original voice, but as a means of amplifying it, allowing his powerful message to resonate with a wider audience. To create this collection I developed a set of custom prompts laying out the rules for AI to follow in modernizing the text. I then directly compared the updated version to the original text sentence by sentence making revisions where needed. The result, I believe, is a faithful and accessible rendering of Wesley's thought, preserving the integrity of his message while removing the barriers of antiquated language.

Whether you are a long-time admirer of Wesley's work or a newcomer eager to explore his influential thought, I invite you to delve into these pages. These modernized texts are ideally suited for personal devotional reading, enriching your quiet time with God. Even more, they are designed to spark vibrant discussion within small groups, Sunday school classes, or any setting where people seek to grow in their faith together. Prepare to be challenged and inspired by the enduring wisdom of John Wesley, now made more accessible than ever before.

It is my sincere hope that you find as much inspiration and spiritual grounding in reading these modernized works as I did in developing them. May they illuminate your understanding of Wesley's legacy and ignite a renewed passion for the Christian faith within your own heart.

AWAKENED WORDS

Context of Wesley's Writing

Eighteenth-century England was a period of stark contrasts, deeply divided between the unparalleled wealth and intellectual ferment enjoyed by the aristocracy and the harsh realities faced by the burgeoning working class. This significant segment of society lived in conditions fostering widespread spiritual and social malaise, creating fertile ground for John Wesley's ministry and the rise of Methodism. The gap between the wealthy landowners, merchants, and professionals and the laborers, farmers, and artisans was immense and deeply ingrained.

The burgeoning Industrial Revolution, though still in its early stages, drew people from rural areas to urban centers like London, Bristol, and Manchester seeking work, leading to overcrowding as cities were ill-equipped to handle the rapid population growth. Housing was scarce, and slums teemed with disease and squalor. Sewage systems were inadequate or non-existent, leading to widespread outbreaks of diseases like typhus, smallpox, and cholera, clean water was a luxury, and public health was virtually unheard of.

Life in rural England was no less challenging, as Enclosure Acts, which consolidated common lands into private ownership, displaced many small farmers and pushed them into poverty or forced them to seek work in the cities. Agricultural laborers faced long hours, low wages, and seasonal unemployment. The working class faced significant economic hardship, characterized by wages that were often insufficient to meet basic needs, especially during periods of economic downturn. Jobs were often unstable, depending on seasonal work, the success of local industries, and wider economic conditions, making poverty a constant threat. Food prices fluctuated wildly, and shortages were common, leading to periods of near starvation. A lack of a strong social safety net meant the existing Poor Laws provided minimal support to the truly destitute, often in harsh and degrading workhouses, with relief being insufficient and stigmatized.

Education was primarily for the wealthy, meaning most working-class children received little or no formal education, limiting their opportunities and perpetuating the cycle of poverty. Brutal working conditions were pervasive, with workers, including children, often laboring for 12-16 hours a day, six days a week, in dangerous and unhealthy environments. Mining, manufacturing, and other industries exposed workers to dangerous machinery, toxic fumes, and the risk of injury or death. Children as young as five or six were employed in factories and mines, often enduring brutal treatment and suffering from long-term health problems.

A moral and spiritual vacuum existed, as the established Church of England was often seen as detached from the lives of the working class. Many parish priests were poorly educated and more concerned with social status than with pastoral care, and services were often formal and inaccessible to the common person. Poverty, despair, and lack of opportunity led to widespread social problems such as alcoholism, gambling, and crime. Many felt trapped in a cycle of poverty and despair, with little hope for a better future in this life.

This created a spiritual vacuum that Methodism was uniquely positioned to fill, emphasizing personal conversion and a direct experience of God's grace, appealing to those who felt alienated from the formality of the established church. Wesley and his followers believed in the importance of social action and actively worked to alleviate poverty and suffering through education, charity, and practical assistance. Methodist preachers travelled extensively, preaching in open fields, barns, and homes, reaching those who would never attend a formal church service.

Methodist societies provided a sense of community and mutual support, offering a network of care and belonging to those who felt isolated and marginalized. Methodism gave the working class a voice and a sense of agency, empowering them to improve their lives and advocate for social change, offering a message of hope and salvation, providing comfort and purpose in the face of hardship and despair. As such, the harsh realities of life for the working class in 18th century England, encompassing poverty, social inequality, economic hardship, and a perceived apathy from the established church, created a desperate need for both spiritual and practical assistance. John Wesley and the Methodist movement emerged as a powerful force, offering a message of hope, community, and social action that resonated deeply with the marginalized and dispossessed, ultimately transforming the religious and social landscape of England.

AWAKENED WORDS

The Nature, Design, and General Rules of Our United Societies

May 1st, 1743

Introduction

This modernized edition of "The Nature, Design, and General Rules of Our United Societies" offers a fascinating glimpse into the very beginnings of the Methodist movement. Written before the name "Methodist" was even widely used, this document lays out the foundational principles of a movement that would have a profound impact.

I find it striking how Wesley emphasizes action and good works right from the start. He focuses on the outward expressions of faith—how we live and interact with others—before addressing inward practices like prayer and Bible study. This focus on a lived faith, a faith demonstrated through concrete actions, is what distinguished the early Methodists. This is unlike other religious movements of the time that typically focused on differences in theology or doctrine. Wesley's beliefs were not very distinct from the prevailing church in his day, the fact he wanted to live his beliefs out in a real everyday way is what made his teaching distinct. These general rules provided a practical framework for personal and social transformation.

I hope this modernized version of the General Rules inspires you to consider how your own faith is expressed in your every day life in real ways.

Summary

In late 1739, John Wesley began meeting with a small group in London seeking spiritual guidance, marking the beginning of the United Society, later known as the Methodist movement. This society, characterized by its emphasis on both outward religious observance and a deeper pursuit of God's grace, spread to America and established a structured system of classes for spiritual growth and accountability. Members committed to "fleeing sin and seeking salvation" were expected to adhere to three general rules, demonstrated through their actions and beliefs. First, do no harm by avoiding a range of evils, including dishonesty, substance abuse, exploitation, conflict, gossip, and extravagant living. Second, do good by meeting the physical and spiritual needs of others, prioritizing fellow believers, and living diligently and thriftily. Third, attend the means of grace through regular worship, engagement with Scripture, communion, prayer, Bible study, and fasting. These rules, based on biblical teachings and illuminated by the Holy Spirit, served as the foundation for Methodist societies, with members held accountable and those who persistently violated the rules subject to removal.

Modernized Text

1. Towards the end of 1739, eight or ten people in London came to me (John Wesley). They were deeply convicted of their sin and desperately seeking redemption. They asked me to pray with them and advise them on how to escape God's judgment, which they felt was imminent. A couple more people joined them the next day with similar requests. To dedicate more time to this important work, I designated a day for us all to meet. We gathered every week, on Thursday evenings. As more people joined us daily, I offered them the advice I felt they needed most. We always ended our meetings with prayers tailored to each person's situation.

This is how the United Society began, first in Europe and then in America. This kind of society is a group of people who outwardly live a religious life and are also seeking a deeper, more powerful experience of God's grace. They unite to pray together, receive encouragement and instruction from the Bible, and lovingly support each other. Their goal is to help one another grow in their faith and find salvation.

2. To help determine whether members are truly growing in their faith, each society is divided into smaller groups called classes, based on where people live. Each class has about twelve people, and one person serves as the leader. The class leader's responsibilities are:

3. To meet with each person in their class at least once a week: (1) to ask about their spiritual well-being; (2) to offer advice, correction, comfort, or encouragement as

needed; (3) to collect any contributions they wish to make for the support of the preachers, the church, and the poor.

4. To meet with the ministers and the society stewards once a week: (1) to inform the minister about anyone who is sick or behaving inappropriately and refuses correction; (2) to give the stewards the money collected from the class during the previous week.

5. There's only one requirement for joining these societies: a desire to escape God's judgment and find salvation from sin. But if this desire is genuine, it will be evident in how you live.

6. Therefore, those who remain in these societies are expected to demonstrate their desire for salvation by, **First: Doing no harm** and avoiding all kinds of evil, especially common practices such as:

• Misusing God's name.

• Dishonoring the Lord's Day by working, buying, or selling.

• Drunkenness: buying, selling, or drinking alcohol, except in emergencies.

• Slaveholding: buying or selling slaves.

• Fighting, arguing, or suing one another; getting revenge; insulting each other; excessive talking while conducting business.

• Buying or selling smuggled goods (goods that haven't paid taxes).

• Charging or paying excessive interest.

• Unkind or pointless gossip; especially criticizing government officials or ministers.

- Treating others in ways we wouldn't want to be treated.
- Doing things we know don't honor God, such as:
- Wearing expensive jewelry and clothes.
- Engaging in entertainment that isn't appropriate for a Christian.
- Singing songs or reading books that don't promote knowledge or love of God.
- Luxurious living and unnecessary self-pampering.
- Hoarding wealth.
- Borrowing money or buying things on credit without being able to repay.

7. Members are also expected to demonstrate their desire for salvation, **Secondly: By doing good;** by being merciful in every way possible; by taking every opportunity to do good to everyone:

To their physical needs, according to the ability God provides, by feeding the hungry, clothing the naked, and visiting or assisting those who are sick or in prison.

To their spiritual needs, by instructing, correcting, or encouraging all those with whom we interact. We reject the idea that we shouldn't do good unless we feel like it.

By doing good, especially to fellow Christians and those seeking faith; by prioritizing them in employment and business dealings, supporting one another, especially because the world will only care for its own.

By being diligent and thrifty, so that the gospel isn't discredited.

By patiently persevering in our faith, denying ourselves, and accepting hardship daily; by being willing to endure criticism for being a Christian, even to the point of being treated like dirt. We should expect that people will falsely accuse us of all kinds of evil because of our faith in Christ.

8. Finally, members are expected to demonstrate their desire for salvation, **Thirdly: By participating in all of God's ordained activities**, such as:
- Attending public worship.
- Engaging with Scripture, whether by reading or hearing it explained.
- Participating in Holy Communion.
- Praying as individuals and families.
- Studying the Bible.
- Fasting or abstaining.

9. These are the General Rules of our societies. We are taught by God to observe these rules through the Bible, which is our ultimate and only guide for belief and action. God's Spirit makes these rules clear to all those whose hearts have been truly awakened. If anyone among us habitually breaks these rules, those responsible for their spiritual care should address the issue. We will warn them about their behavior and patiently support them for a time. But if they don't change, they can no longer be part of our community. By doing this, we protect our own spiritual integrity.

Key Points

- **The origin of the United Societies:** The societies began organically in London with small groups seeking spiritual guidance and support from John Wesley.
- **Purpose of the societies:** These groups aimed to foster spiritual growth, encourage mutual accountability, and help members find salvation.
- **Class meetings:** Smaller groups within the societies, led by a class leader, provided more personal care and support. Leaders inquired about spiritual well-being, offered guidance, and collected contributions.
- **Membership requirement:** The sole requirement for joining was a desire to escape God's judgment and find salvation. This desire, however, was expected to manifest in a changed life.
- **Doing no harm:** Members were expected to abstain from various harmful behaviors, including misuse of God's name, Sabbath-breaking, drunkenness, slaveholding, interpersonal conflict, unfair business practices, gossip, and frivolous living.
- **Doing good:** Members were to actively engage in acts of mercy, both physical and spiritual, prioritizing fellow Christians and demonstrating diligence and thriftiness.
- **Staying connected to God:** Members were expected to participate in public worship, Scripture engagement, Holy Communion, prayer, Bible study, and fasting.
- **Discipline and accountability:** Those who habitually broke the rules were to be warned and lovingly supported. Unrepentant members were to be removed from the society to protect its integrity.

Personal Reflection Questions

- How does my life reflect the values outlined in the General Rules? Are there areas where I need to make changes to align my behavior with my desire for salvation?
- Am I actively involved in a community of faith where I can receive support and offer encouragement to others? Do I have people in my life who hold me accountable for my spiritual growth?
- Do I prioritize acts of mercy and compassion, both physical and spiritual? Am I diligent and thrifty in my use of resources?
- Am I faithfully engaging in the spiritual practices such as prayer, Scripture study, and worship?

Prayer Prompts

Morning: "Lord, help me to live according to your will today. Reveal any areas where I am falling short of the standards outlined in your Word. Give me the strength to resist temptation and to actively pursue good works. Thank you for the gift of community and accountability."

Evening: "God, I thank you for your grace and mercy. I confess that I have not always lived up to your expectations. Forgive me for my shortcomings and help me to grow in holiness. I ask for your guidance and support as I strive to follow you more closely. Help me to be a blessing to others, both in word and deed."

Advice to a People Called Methodist

Oct 10th, 1745

Introduction

"Advice for People Called Methodist," is a pivotal document in Methodist history. It marks a turning point where Wesley, rather than rejecting the label "Methodist"—a term initially used derisively—embraces it and redefines its meaning. He speaks directly to those drawn to this nascent movement, defining "Methodists" not by what others assume about them, but by their own pursuit of holiness, rooted in love for God and neighbor, and their core beliefs in faith, grace, and the Holy Spirit. He acknowledges their unique situation: a new movement, distinct in name, doctrine, and practice, drawn from diverse backgrounds, and committed to their existing churches despite resistance.

Wesley warns them against expecting universal acceptance, recognizing their beliefs and practices would cause offense. He urges resilience in the face of criticism, emphasizing humility, love, and reliance on God. He offers practical guidance: focus on spiritual growth, avoid dwelling on negativity, and maintain unity while respecting differing views.

This advice, forged in the crucible of early Methodism, remains relevant for anyone seeking a faithful life. It reminds us that discipleship often demands courage, resilience, and unwavering commitment to love and grace —and that sometimes, the best way to disarm your critics is to own the very label they intended as an insult, transforming it into a badge of honor.

Summary

Methodism, as defined by John Wesley, is characterized by a pursuit of holiness, both inwardly and outwardly, aligning thoughts, words, and actions with God's will. This pursuit stems from a love for God, grounded in faith, which is a gift from the Holy Spirit and provides assurance of God's mercy and forgiveness through Christ. Methodists strive to emulate God's qualities of justice, mercy, and truth, expressing this through universal love and a commitment to both avoiding evil and actively doing good. This commitment, combined with their unique practices and newly formed, unified community, often leads to misunderstanding and opposition.

Wesley advises Methodists to embrace their unique identity and remain true to their principles, even when facing persecution. He encourages them to trust in God's strength, avoid dwelling on their suffering, and respond to opposition with love and prayer rather than anger or resentment. He emphasizes the importance of maintaining humility, diligently pursuing spiritual growth, and valuing correct doctrine while respecting the freedom of conscience of others. Ultimately, Wesley urges Methodists to prioritize their relationship with Christ above all else, standing firm in their faith and enduring hardship with the courage of true champions.

Modernized Text

Disce, docendus adhuc quæ censet amiculus. -- HOR.

Learn, since you are still needing to be taught, the things which your dear friend thinks. - Horace (Roman Poet)

1. By "Methodists," I mean people who strive to live holy lives, both inwardly and outwardly. They seek to align their thoughts, words, and actions with God's revealed will as found in the Bible. They believe that true religion means becoming more like God—imitating His character and qualities, especially His justice, mercy, and truth. This can be summarized as a universal love that fills their hearts and guides their lives.

2. You, my audience, believe that true love for humanity must come from loving God. You understand that it's impossible to genuinely love every person—even those unrelated by blood or any social connection—unless that love stems from a grateful, childlike love for God, the Father of us all. We see God not just as our personal Father, but as the creator of every human spirit, the loving parent and friend of all people, both in heaven and on earth.

3. You believe this love for God comes only from faith, which you understand as a supernatural confidence in unseen realities. For someone with faith:

> Things beyond our limited senses,
> Invisible to human reason,
> Are clearly revealed as divine.

Faith illuminates and makes real what was hidden.
Doubts and uncertainties vanish,
God, who is invisible, becomes visible
And is experienced by us.[1]

4. You believe this faith involves a certainty that God is merciful to me, a sinner; that God has reconciled humanity to Godself through the death of Jesus Christ, and now accepts me because of Jesus. You define genuine Christian faith as a firm trust and confidence in God (going beyond simply believing the Bible). This trust assures believers that their sins are forgiven and that they are restored to a right relationship with God through Christ's sacrifice.

5. Furthermore, you believe that both faith and love are gifts from the Holy Spirit. In fact, you believe that no one can have any good intentions, desires, or even a single good thought unless it comes from God's power and the inspiration of the Holy Spirit.

6. If you live by these principles, continually striving to know, love, become like, and obey God, the Father of our Lord Jesus Christ, the God of love and forgiveness; if, because of your loving, obedient faith, you diligently avoid all evil and do good to everyone whenever possible, whether friend or enemy; and finally, if you come together to support and encourage each other in your spiritual

---

[1] Originally a verse from "AUTHOR OF FAITH, ETERNAL WORD" a hymn by Charles Wesley

growth, lovingly holding each other accountable, then you are who I mean by "Methodists."

7. My first and most important piece of advice for each of you is this: Carefully and regularly consider your unique circumstances.

8. One of these circumstances is that you are a new movement. Your name, "Methodist," is new, at least in a religious context. It was unheard of just a few years ago, both in our own nation and elsewhere. Your beliefs are also new in that no other group among us, and possibly in the entire Christian world, holds all of them with the same emphasis and interconnectedness. You strongly and consistently emphasize the absolute necessity of complete holiness in heart and life; a peaceful, joyful love for God; a confident trust in unseen realities; an inner assurance of being God's children; and the Holy Spirit's inspiration for every good thought, word, and deed. Perhaps no other group, at least not one so visibly united, places as much emphasis as you do on correct beliefs, outward forms of worship, and participation in the practices that you recognize as coming from God. You place a high value on correct beliefs, earnestly desiring to understand the truth in all things and gladly using every available means to achieve this. However, you don't condemn anyone simply for disagreeing with you, and certainly not assuming that God condemns them for this, as long as they are honest and sincere in their hearts.

9. You highly value the forms of worship in which you were raised, but not so much that it diminishes your love for those who conscientiously disagree with you on these matters. Similarly, you believe participating in the practices

you recognize as God-given is essential to your salvation and that willfully neglecting them would be harmful. However, you don't judge those who hold different beliefs; you don't condemn those who abstain from these practices because they believe they are not commanded by God.

10. Your overall strictness of life can also be considered new. I'm referring to your commitment to abstaining from popular entertainments, including plays, novels, and humorous books; avoiding lighthearted songs and frivolous conversation; your simple style of dress; your ethical business practices; your careful observance of the Sabbath; your conscientiousness regarding paying taxes; your complete avoidance of alcohol (except when medically necessary); and your rule against gossiping, especially about ministers or those in authority. These practices, taken together, can rightly be called new. While some people might be scrupulous about certain aspects of their lives, and others might be strict about different things, there isn't another group that upholds all of these standards together. Therefore, in terms of your name, beliefs, and practices, you can be seen as a distinct, new movement.

11. Another unique aspect of your situation is that you are a newly formed group, recently gathered, or still in the process of gathering, from various other churches and communities. Moreover, you exist without worldly power or influence (being seen as ordinary and unimportant), without wealth (most of you being poor and having only basic necessities), and without exceptional natural talents

or formal education. Even most of your preachers are unschooled and lacking in worldly knowledge.

12. Here's another circumstance unique to you: When other new religious groups form, they typically separate from their previous churches or communities. You, however, do not. In fact, you explicitly reject any desire to separate. You openly and consistently state that you have no such intention and never have. Furthermore, while other established churches usually try to prevent new groups from breaking away, the churches you currently belong to are actively trying to force you out, to create the very division you strongly oppose.

13. Given your unique circumstances, my second piece of advice is this: Don't expect to avoid offending people. Your very name, "Methodist," makes that impossible. Most people who use the term have no idea what it actually means. To them, it's just a strange, foreign-sounding word. They assume it means something bad—a Catholic, a heretic, someone who undermines the Church, or some kind of monstrous person. And as the name spreads, it's likely to pick up even more negative connotations. Therefore, it's pointless for anyone called a Methodist to try to avoid causing offense.

14. Your principles will offend people even more than your name. You'll offend those who rigidly adhere to specific doctrines, forms of worship, and rituals by not emphasizing them as much as they do, and you'll offend those who oppose such things by emphasizing them as much as you do. You'll offend those focused on outward appearances by emphasizing the inner power of faith. You'll offend those who consider themselves moral without

faith by declaring faith essential for God's acceptance. You'll offend those who rely solely on reason by speaking of inspiration and the Holy Spirit. You'll offend those engaging in harmful behaviors like drunkenness, disregarding the Sabbath, and using foul language by avoiding their company and disapproving of their actions. Your lifestyle itself will be a constant offense: your sobriety to those who drink heavily; your serious conversations to those who are frivolous and disrespectful. Many will be offended that you have become so particular, so different, so seemingly strict, questioning so many things they consider harmless and feeling obligated to do so many things they deem unnecessary. This will inevitably offend many, especially your friends and family. Therefore, you must choose between abandoning your principles or giving up the hope of pleasing everyone.

15. What makes your principles even more offensive to some is your unity as a group. This unity makes you more visible and noticeable, leading to suspicion that you're plotting something sinister, especially among those unaware of your unwavering loyalty to the King. Your unity can also seem threatening to those who are easily frightened and believe you have such hidden motives. It makes you more objectionable to those who are passionate about their own beliefs, if that passion is anything other than a genuine love for God and humanity.

16. This offense will be even more deeply felt because you are drawn from so many different churches. The passionate members of those churches will likely believe you despise them and their pastors, perhaps even assuming you think they cannot be saved. This offense is

particularly acute now because you are a newly forming group, and they don't know how large you will grow. Their fear of losing members intensifies their hostility and fuels their anger and resentment.

17. Furthermore, you don't completely leave their churches; you still consider yourselves members. To those who don't understand that you do this out of conscience, this is also irritating. They wish you would just disappear, but as long as you remain, you are a constant irritant.

And what angers them even further is that you lack power, wealth, and formal education, yet despite their resources and influence, they are unable to stop your growth.

18. You should expect the constant offense caused by these various provocations to escalate into hatred, malice, and other forms of unkindness. Those who feel this way will inevitably portray you to others as they see you — as crazy, foolish, or even wicked people unfit to live. The likely human consequence is that, along with your reputation, you will lose the affection of your friends, family, and acquaintances, even those who once loved you deeply. Then you may lose your livelihoods, as people refuse to employ or do business with you. Eventually, unless God intervenes, you could even face danger to your health, freedom, and lives.

19. What further advice can be offered in such a situation? My third piece of advice is this: Ask yourself, "Is the God I serve able to protect me? I cannot rescue myself from these difficulties, much less endure them. I don't know how I could bear losing my reputation, my friends, my possessions, my freedom, or even my life. Can God

give me the strength to face these losses with joy? Can I trust that God will be with me? Does God care for even the smallest details of my life? Does God ever abandon those who trust in God?" Consider this carefully. If you can trust God with everything, then continue forward with the strength God provides.

20. My fourth and earnest piece of advice is this: Stay on the path you are currently following. Remain true to your principles. Never return to a lifeless, outward form of religion. Strive with all your strength for inward and outward holiness, consistently imitating the God you worship and becoming ever more like God in God's character of justice, mercy, and truth.

21. Let your faith be courageous, noble, and generous, far removed from the pettiness of empty rituals—doing things God hasn't commanded or avoiding things God hasn't prohibited—and from the narrowness of bigotry, which limits our love to our own group or viewpoint. Above all, remain firm in your obedient faith, faith in the God of forgiving mercy, the God and Father of our Lord Jesus Christ, who has loved you and given himself for you. Give God credit for all the good you find within yourselves: your peace, joy, and love; your strength to do God's will and endure hardship, all through the power of the Holy Spirit. At the same time, be careful to avoid fanaticism. Don't attribute human imaginings to the all-wise God. Don't expect guidance or strength from God except through diligently using the means God has provided, such as prayer, Scripture, and Christian community.

22. Remain true to your principles regarding doctrines and outward religious practices. Participate in the

practices that you believe are ordained by God, but avoid being judgmental towards those who do not. Follow the forms of worship you find meaningful, yet love those who cannot conform as fellow Christians. Value sound doctrine so that your beliefs, as much as possible, align with truth and reason. But guard against anger, dislike, or contempt toward those who hold different views. You are constantly accused of such judgmental attitudes (and what aren't you accused of?), but be careful not to give any credence to these accusations. Don't condemn anyone for disagreeing with you. Respect everyone's freedom of thought and conscience. Let everyone use their own judgment, as each person is accountable to God. Reject any form of persecution, whether subtle or overt. If you can't persuade someone through reason and love, never try to coerce them. If love doesn't draw them in, leave them to God, who judges all.

23. Don't expect others to treat you with the same respect. Some will try to scare you away from your beliefs; others will try to shame you into adopting a more conventional faith, mocking and ridiculing your distinctiveness. But the greatest danger will come from those who use different tactics: gentle persuasion, apparent kindness, and earnest expressions of goodwill (which may be genuine). In these situations, it's crucial to avoid even the appearance of anger, contempt, or unkindness while firmly holding onto your beliefs and practices.

24. Your refusal to participate in sinful or frivolous activities will likely be misinterpreted as coldness or unkindness by your former acquaintances. This is a

burden you must accept. However, strive to avoid any genuine unkindness, including harsh or disrespectful language, aloofness, or unusual behavior. Speak to them with as much tenderness and love, and behave with as much courtesy and kindness, as you can, being careful not to cause unnecessary offense to anyone, whether neighbor or stranger, friend or foe.

25. My fifth piece of advice is this: Avoid dwelling on your suffering, on the persecution you've endured, and the wickedness of those who persecute you. Nothing angers them more. While there may be times when these things must be discussed, make it a general rule to speak of them as little as your conscience allows. Talking about your persecution tends to inflame your opponents and can appear like boasting or self-importance. It can also lead to pride, making you think too highly of yourselves. It can stir up or intensify resentment, anger, and other negative feelings in your hearts. At best, it's a waste of time; instead of focusing on the wickedness of others, you could be focusing on the goodness of God. At worst, it's a deliberate sin: gossiping, backbiting, speaking ill of others —a sin you must constantly guard against, as it can creep in unnoticed in countless ways. Wouldn't it be far better for your souls, instead of speaking against them, to pray for them? Strengthen your love for those who oppose you, those you believe are fighting against God, by earnestly praying for them, that God may open their eyes and transform their hearts.

26. Finally, I entrust you to the care of God, who has all power in heaven and on earth. I pray that in every situation you may stand firm and resilient, like an anvil under the

hammer. I pray that you will value nothing in this world above your relationship with Christ, considering everything else as worthless in comparison. And always remember: true champions are willing to endure any hardship, even the most extreme suffering, in order to achieve victory in Christ.

Key Points

- *Methodists are defined by their pursuit of holiness:* It's not just a name, but a commitment to aligning thoughts, words, and actions with God's will, characterized by love for God and humanity.
- *Faith is the foundation of love:* Love for others flows from a grateful, childlike love for God, rooted in a supernatural confidence in unseen realities and the assurance of God's mercy through Christ.
- *The Methodist movement is unique:* Its newness, emphasis on both inward and outward holiness, combination of doctrinal conviction with tolerance for differing views, and commitment to remaining within established churches distinguish it.
- *Expect offense and persecution:* The name, principles, unity, and diverse membership of the Methodists will inevitably lead to misunderstanding, criticism, and even hostility from various groups.
- *Trust in God's protection:* Facing potential losses and hardships requires complete trust in God's ability to sustain and deliver.
- *Maintain your principles, avoid fanaticism and judgmentalism:* Stay true to your beliefs and practices, but avoid rigid legalism, attributing human opinions to God, or condemning those who disagree.
- *Focus on God's goodness, pray for opponents:* Resist dwelling on suffering and persecution. Instead, focus on God's goodness and actively pray for those who oppose you.

Personal Reflection Questions

- How does my life reflect the Methodist emphasis on both inward and outward holiness? Are there areas where I am compromising my principles or neglecting spiritual growth?
- Do I truly love God with all my heart, soul, mind, and strength? Does this love motivate my actions and relationships?
- Am I prepared to face potential criticism and hardship for following Christ? Do I trust in God's protection and provision?
- Am I careful to avoid judgmentalism and fanaticism? Do I extend grace and understanding to those who hold different views?

Prayer Prompts

Morning: "Lord, help me to live a life of true holiness, reflecting your love and grace in all I do. Strengthen my faith and give me the courage to stand firm in my convictions, even in the face of opposition. Protect me from pride and judgmentalism, and fill me with your perfect love."

Evening: "God, I thank you for your faithfulness and the call to follow you completely. I confess that I sometimes struggle with fear and doubt. Help me to trust in your protection and to focus on your goodness. I lift up to you those who oppose me, asking that you would open their eyes to the truth and transform their hearts. Help me to love them as you love them."

AWAKENED WORDS

Wesley's Rules for Singing

1761

Introduction

John Wesley and his brother Charles understood that congregational singing was a critical part of Christian gathering and worship. During their lifetimes they authored thousands of hymns, many of which are in regular use today. The expected those part of the Methodist movement to take their spiritual lives seriously including down to how intentionally they sang, which was a large part of any Methodist gathering. These rules below first appeared in a book of hymns produced for Methodist worship. To focus is on the communal nature of this type of singing which differentiated it from other forms of musical performance.

Modernized Text

1. Learn these hymns first. Afterward, you can learn as many others as you like.

2. Sing them exactly as written here, without changing them. If you've learned them differently, unlearn that way as soon as possible.

3. Sing along! Join in with the congregation as often as you can. Don't let minor fatigue or weariness stop you. If it feels like a sacrifice, embrace it, and you'll be blessed.

4. Sing heartily and with enthusiasm. Don't sing as if you're half-dead or half-asleep. Sing out with strength and confidence. Don't be afraid to let your voice be heard, any more than you were when you sang secular songs.

5. Sing with humility. Don't shout so that you overpower the rest of the congregation and ruin the harmony. Blend your voice with others to create a unified, beautiful sound.

6. Sing in rhythm. Keep pace with the music. Don't sing ahead or lag behind. Pay attention to the leading voices and follow them as precisely as you can. Don't sing too slowly. That dragging tempo tends to creep in when people get lazy. It's time to get rid of that habit and sing with the same energy and tempo as when we first learned the songs.

7. Sing with a focus on God. Pay attention to the meaning of every word. Aim to please God more than yourself or anyone else. Focus on the message of the hymn, not just the melody. Continually offer your heart to God as you sing. Then your singing will be pleasing to God now, and God will reward you in the future.

Introduction to Wesley's Sermons

An Introduction

John Wesley's sermons stand as a cornerstone of Methodist theology and practice, offering invaluable insights into the heart of this dynamic movement.

These written versions, often published as small, accessible tracts, represent the distillation of Wesley's powerful preaching. While we recognize that the spoken word, delivered with his characteristic fervor, may have differed slightly, these published sermons provide the most reliable record of his theological development. The three sermons that follow are considered among his most important, each offering a deep exploration of a key theme within Methodist doctrine. Spanning different periods of the movement's growth, they illuminate the evolution of Wesley's thought and provide some of the clearest definitions we have of what constitutes genuine Methodist belief. They are essential reading for anyone seeking to understand the roots and enduring principles of Methodism.

AWAKENED WORDS

The Almost Christian

July 26, 1741

Introduction

This sermon offers a fascinating glimpse into the early stages of the Methodist movement. Preached relatively early in his ministry, John Wesley grapples with the very essence of what it means to be a Christian, seeking to articulate what would distinguish this burgeoning group from others who might also appear outwardly devout. He delves into the critical distinction between a superficial adherence to Christian principles and a truly transformative faith, a distinction that would become a hallmark of Methodist theology and practice. Wesley's exploration of the "almost Christian" and the "completely Christian" isn't merely an academic exercise; it's a deeply personal and pastoral reflection on the nature of genuine discipleship.

As we consider Wesley's words, it's easy to feel overwhelmed. Even the standard he sets for the "almost Christian"—with its emphasis on integrity, outward godliness, and sincerity—can seem daunting, perhaps even unattainable. The prospect of being a completely Christian, with its all-encompassing love for God and neighbor, and its unwavering faith, might feel ridiculously out of reach. Wesley fully understands this struggle. He recognizes the immense challenge he lays before us. But he also understands that we are not called to achieve this transformation through our own strength alone. This sermon isn't about setting an impossible standard to discourage us. It's about pointing us to the God who is able to do what we cannot do for ourselves. It's about recognizing that true Christian living is not about striving in our own power, but about partnering with the transformative grace of God, who empowers us to love, to believe, and to live in a way that reflects the very character of Christ.

Summary

"The Almost Christian" explores the critical difference between a superficial adherence to Christianity and true, transformative faith. John Wesley begins by outlining what it means to be almost a Christian, emphasizing outward displays of integrity (honesty, justice, basic kindness), an appearance of godliness (avoiding sinful behaviors, engaging in good works, participating in religious practices), and sincerity (a genuine intention to serve God). Wesley argues that many people reach this level, yet it's insufficient.

He then delves into what constitutes a complete Christian. This involves more than outward actions; it requires a deep, all-encompassing love for God and a similar love for all people, even enemies. Crucially, it includes true Christian faith – not just intellectual assent to doctrine, but a confident trust in Christ's sacrifice for forgiveness and reconciliation with God. This faith purifies the heart and motivates a life of love and service.

Wesley uses his own past as an example, admitting he was once "almost" a Christian despite his outward piety and sincere intentions. He concludes by urging his listeners to examine their own hearts: Do they possess this all-encompassing love for God and neighbor? Do they have true faith in Christ? He warns against complacency and encourages them to strive for a complete, transformative faith, marked by love, joy, and the assurance of God's grace. He emphasizes that without this genuine faith and love, a person's life, regardless of outward appearances, is ultimately in vain.

Modernized Text

"You almost persuade me to be a Christian."
Acts 26:28

Many people go this far. Ever since Christianity began, there have been countless individuals in every time and place who have been almost persuaded to become Christians. But since it means nothing to God to only go part of the way, it's crucial to consider:

First: What does it mean to be almost a Christian?
Second: What does it mean to be a Christian completely?

1. Being almost a Christian implies, first, basic integrity. I assume everyone agrees with this, especially since by "basic integrity" I mean the kind of honesty that wasn't just recommended by classical philosophers, but expected among everyday people, and often practiced by them. According to these principles, people should be just, not stealing from their neighbors through robbery or theft, not oppressing the poor or using extortion, not cheating or deceiving anyone in business dealings, not depriving anyone of their rights, and, if possible, avoiding debt.

2. Furthermore, basic integrity included respecting truth as well as justice. So, people despised not only those who swore falsely, calling upon God to witness a lie, but also those known to slander or falsely accuse others. They viewed deliberate liars of any kind as little better, considering them a disgrace to humanity and a menace to society.

3. Moreover, a certain degree of love and support was expected among people. They expected people to help each other, as long as it didn't harm themselves. This

extended beyond simple acts of kindness that cost nothing. It included feeding the hungry if they had extra food, clothing the naked with spare clothes, and generally giving those in need whatever they didn't require themselves. This, at a minimum, was what basic integrity looked like: the first component of being almost a Christian.

4. A second aspect of being almost a Christian is having an outward appearance of godliness, following the ethical guidelines prescribed in the Gospels—having the external characteristics of a true Christian. So, the almost Christian avoids anything the Gospels forbid. They don't misuse God's name. They bless instead of curse. They don't make vows at all, simply letting their "yes" be "yes" and their "no" be "no." They don't ignore the Lord's Day, or allow it to be ignored, even by visitors. They avoid not only adultery, fornication, and sexual impurity, but also any word or look that could lead to those things. They abstain from all idle words, including gossip, backbiting, and "coarse joking" and, in short, from any conversation that isn't "helpful for building others up," conversation that would "grieve the Holy Spirit of God, with whom you were sealed for the day of redemption."

5. They avoid drunkenness, wild parties, and gluttony. They avoid, as much as possible, all conflict and contention, continually striving to live peacefully with everyone. If wronged, they don't seek revenge or retaliate. They don't insult, quarrel, or mock others, whether for their flaws or weaknesses. They don't intentionally harm or upset anyone. In all their actions and words, they follow

the simple rule: "Do to others what you would have them do to you."

6. And in doing good, they don't limit themselves to simple acts of kindness. They work hard and even endure hardship to benefit others, seeking to help in any way they can. Despite fatigue or discomfort, "whatever their hand finds to do, they do it with all their might," whether for friends or enemies, good or evil. They are "not lazy" in any endeavor. As they "have opportunity," they do "good" in every way possible "to all people," attending to their spiritual as well as physical needs. They correct the wicked, instruct the ignorant, strengthen the wavering, encourage the good, and comfort the suffering. They strive to awaken those who are spiritually asleep, to lead those whom God has already awakened to the "fountain opened to cleanse them from sin and impurity," and to encourage those saved through faith to live in a way that reflects well on the gospel of Christ.

7. Those who have the outward form of godliness also utilize the means of grace, engaging in all of them whenever possible. They regularly attend church, but not like those who come into God's presence adorned with excessive jewelry and expensive clothing, or with gaudy and vain attire. These people, through their inappropriate socializing or frivolous behavior, demonstrate that they lack both the form and the power of godliness. I wish we didn't have some among us who are guilty of the same! They may enter the church looking around distractedly or with signs of listless indifference, even though they may briefly pray for God's blessing on what they are about to do. During the worship service, they may fall asleep,

recline in a comfortable position, or, as if God were asleep, chat with each other or look around as if they have nothing to do. These people shouldn't even claim to have the form of godliness! No, someone with even the outward appearance of godliness behaves with seriousness and attentiveness throughout the service. Especially when approaching the Lord's Table, they don't act carelessly or flippantly, but with a demeanor that expresses nothing but "God, have mercy on me, a sinner!"

8. In addition to this, if those who lead households regularly hold family prayers and set aside time for private prayer, displaying consistent seriousness in their daily lives, then they have the outward form of godliness. Only one thing more is needed for them to be almost a Christian: sincerity.

9. By sincerity, I mean a genuine, internal religious motivation that drives these outward actions. Without this, we don't even possess basic pagan integrity, not even enough to satisfy a pagan Epicurean poet. Even that miserable person, in his more rational moments, could attest that...

> *Oderunt peccare boni, virtutis amore;*
> *Oderunt peccare mali, formidine poenae.*
> [Good people avoid sin from the love of virtue;
> Wicked men avoid sin from a fear of punishment.]

So if someone avoids doing wrong only to escape punishment ("Non pasces in cruce corvos" — "You won't feed the crows on a cross," meaning "You won't be hanged"), that, as the pagan would say, "is its own reward." Even he wouldn't consider someone like that a good pagan. Therefore, if anyone, motivated by fear of punishment, loss of friends, financial setbacks, or a damaged reputation, not only refrains from evil but does much good and diligently uses all the means of grace, we still couldn't accurately call that person even almost a Christian. Without a better motivation in their heart, they are simply a complete hypocrite.

10. Therefore, sincerity is absolutely essential to being almost a Christian. This means a genuine intention to serve God and a heartfelt desire to do God's will. It necessarily implies a sincere aim to please God in everything—in all conversations, actions, and decisions. If someone is almost a Christian, this intention permeates their entire life. It's the underlying motivation for doing good, avoiding evil, and participating in religious practices.

11. But you might ask, "Is it possible for someone to go this far and still only be almost a Christian? What more could being a completely Christian involve?" I answer: First, I know it's possible to go this far and yet not be a full Christian, not just from the Bible, but from personal experience.

12. Friends, I speak to you with great candor. "Forgive me this wrong" if I openly share my own past failings for your benefit and for the sake of the gospel. Allow me to speak freely about myself as if I were talking about someone else. I'm willing to humble myself so that you may be uplifted, and to become even more insignificant for the glory of my Lord.

13. For years, I went this far, as many here can attest. I diligently avoided evil and strived to maintain a clear conscience, making the most of my time and seizing every opportunity to do good to everyone. I consistently and carefully engaged in all public and private religious practices, striving for consistent seriousness in my conduct at all times and in all places. And, God is my witness, I did all this sincerely, with a genuine intention to serve God, a heartfelt desire to do God's will in everything, to please God who called me to "fight the good fight" and "take hold of eternal life." Yet my own conscience, guided by the Holy Spirit, testifies that during all that time, I was only almost a Christian.

You might ask: "What more is involved in being a completely Christian?" I answer:

14. First: Love for God. As Scripture says, "Love the Lord your God with all your heart, with all your soul, with all your mind, and with all your strength." This kind of love consumes the entire heart, stirs up all affections, fills the soul to its capacity, and utilizes all its faculties to their fullest extent. Someone who loves God this way constantly "rejoices in God their Savior." Their delight is in the Lord, their Lord and their All, to whom they "give thanks in everything." Their whole desire is for God and the remembrance of God's name. Their heart constantly cries out, "Whom have I in heaven but you? And earth has nothing I desire besides you." What could they desire besides God? Not the world or its attractions, for they are "crucified to the world, and the world to them." They are crucified to "the lust of the flesh, the lust of the eyes, and

the pride of life." Indeed, they are dead to all pride, because "love does not boast." But those who live in love, live in God, and God in them, and are insignificant in their own eyes.

15. Second: Love for our neighbors. As our Lord said, "Love your neighbor as yourself." If you ask, "Who is my neighbor?", we answer: Every person in the world, every child of God, who is the Father of all spirits. We cannot exclude even our enemies or those who are enemies of God and their own souls. Every Christian loves these people as they love themselves, "as Christ loved us." To fully understand this love, consider Paul's description: it is "patient and kind." It "does not envy." It doesn't judge rashly. It "is not proud," but makes the one who loves the least, the servant of all. Love "is not rude," but "becomes all things to all people." It "is not self-seeking," but seeks only the good of others, that they may be saved. "Love is not easily angered." It casts out wrath, which those who have are lacking in love. "It keeps no record of wrongs." It "does not rejoice in evil, but rejoices with the truth." It "always protects, always trusts, always hopes, always perseveres."

16. One more essential element, though inseparable from the previous two, completes the picture of a completely Christian: faith. Scripture speaks powerfully of this: "Everyone who believes is born of God," says the beloved disciple. "To all who did receive him, to those who believed in his name, he gave the right to become children of God." And "this is the victory that has overcome the world, even our faith." Indeed, our Lord declares,

"Whoever believes in the Son has eternal life and will not be condemned; they have crossed over from death to life."

17. But let's not deceive ourselves. "It must be carefully noted that the faith which does not lead to repentance, love, and good works is not true, living faith, but a dead and devilish one." Even demons believe that Christ was born of a virgin, performed miracles, declared himself God, suffered a painful death to redeem us from eternal death, rose again, ascended to heaven, sits at God's right hand, and will return to judge the living and the dead. Demons believe these core doctrines, and they believe everything written in the Old and New Testaments. Yet despite this, they are still demons, remaining in their damnable state because they lack true Christian faith.

18. True Christian faith, according to our Church, is "not only believing that Holy Scripture and the Articles of our Faith are true, but also having a sure trust and confidence of being saved from everlasting damnation by Christ." It is "a sure trust and confidence that a person has in God, that through the merits of Christ, their sins are forgiven, and they are reconciled to God, which results in a loving heart to obey God's commandments."

19. Whoever possesses this faith—a faith that "purifies the heart" (through God's power dwelling within) from "pride, anger, desire, all unrighteousness, all filthiness of flesh and spirit," and fills it with a love stronger than death, both for God and for all people; a love that motivates them to do God's work, gladly spending and being spent for others, and enduring with joy not only the reproach of Christ—being mocked, despised, and hated—but also whatever suffering God allows people or demons to inflict

—whoever has this faith working through love is not just almost, but completely, a Christian.

20. But who are the living examples of these things? I implore you, friends, as in the presence of God, before whom "hell and destruction lie uncovered—how much more human hearts!"—ask your own hearts: "Am I one of them? Do I practice justice, mercy, and truth to the extent that even pagan integrity demands? If so, do I have the outward form of a Christian, the appearance of godliness? Do I abstain from evil—from everything forbidden in God's Word? Whatever good I find to do, do I do it with all my might? Do I earnestly engage in all the means of grace at every opportunity? And is all of this done with a sincere intention and desire to please God in everything?"

21. Aren't many of you aware that you've never even come this far? That you've never been even almost a Christian? That you haven't lived up to the standards of basic integrity, let alone the outward form of Christian godliness? And that God hasn't seen sincerity in you, a genuine intention to please God in everything? You've never even tried to dedicate all your words, works, business, studies, and recreation to God's glory. You've never even intended or desired that whatever you did should be done "in the name of the Lord Jesus," and as such, be "a spiritual sacrifice, acceptable to God through Christ."

22. But even if you have, do good intentions and good desires make someone a Christian? Certainly not, unless they lead to action. As someone said, "Hell is paved with good intentions." So the most important question remains: Is God's love poured out into your heart? Can you cry out,

"My God, and my All"? Do you desire nothing but God? Are you happy in God? Is God your glory, your delight, your crown of rejoicing? And is this commandment written on your heart: "Whoever loves God must also love their brother and sister"? Do you then love your neighbor as yourself? Do you love everyone—even your enemies, even the enemies of God—as you love your own soul, as Christ loved you? And do you believe that Christ loved you and gave himself for you? Do you have faith in Christ's blood? Do you believe that the Lamb of God has taken away your sins and thrown them into the depths of the sea, that Christ has cancelled the debt that stood against you, taking it away, nailing it to his cross? Do you truly have redemption through Christ's blood, the forgiveness of your sins? And does the Holy Spirit testify with your spirit that you are a child of God?

23. The God and Father of our Lord Jesus Christ, who stands in our midst, knows that if anyone dies without this faith and this love, it would have been better if they had never been born. Wake up, then, you who are sleeping, and call on God! Call now while God may be found. Don't let God rest until God makes his "goodness pass before you," until God proclaims to you his name: "The Lord, the Lord God, compassionate and gracious, slow to anger, abounding in love and faithfulness, maintaining love to thousands, and forgiving wickedness, rebellion and sin." Don't let anyone persuade you with empty words to settle for less than this prize to which God has called you. But cry out to God day and night, who "while we were still powerless, died for the ungodly," until you know in whom you have believed and can say, "My Lord, and my God!"

Remember always to pray and never give up until you can lift up your hands to heaven and declare to the one who lives forever and ever, "Lord, you know everything; you know that I love you."

24. May we all experience what it means to be not just almost, but completely, Christians, justified freely by God's grace through the redemption that is in Jesus, knowing we have peace with God through Jesus Christ, rejoicing in the hope of God's glory, and having God's love poured into our hearts through the Holy Spirit who has been given to us!

Key points

- *Almost Christian is not enough:* Many people possess outward morality, even religious zeal, but lack the core transformation of a truly Christian life.
- *Basic integrity is the foundation:* Honesty, justice, and a degree of love for others are essential, even for basic human decency. This is the starting point, not the destination.
- *Outward godliness is necessary but insufficient:* Avoiding sinful behaviors and engaging in religious practices are important, but they must flow from genuine inward transformation, not hypocrisy.
- *Sincerity is crucial:* A genuine intention to serve God and desire to do God's will are essential for being almost a Christian. Hypocrisy, even with good actions, is insufficient.
- *Complete Christianity involves love and faith:* A truly Christian life is characterized by a deep love for God (consuming the whole heart) and a love for all people (even enemies). This love is rooted in a genuine faith in Christ, including assurance of salvation and a transformed heart.
- *Faith works through love:* True faith isn't just intellectual assent; it's a living faith that transforms the heart and overflows in love for God and others.

Personal Reflection Questions

- Where do I fall on the spectrum of being "almost" and "completely" Christian? Are there areas of my life where I am relying on outward appearances rather than inward transformation?
- Is my motivation for doing good rooted in a genuine love for God and others, or is it driven by other factors like fear of punishment or desire for approval?
- Do I have a deep, personal assurance of my salvation through Christ? How is this assurance impacting my life and relationships?

Prayer Prompts

Morning: "Lord, help me to examine my heart and motivations today. Reveal any areas where I am only 'almost' a Christian. Cultivate in me a genuine love for you and for others, and strengthen my faith in your grace. May my actions flow from a heart transformed by your love."

Evening: "God, I thank you for your unwavering love and the call to a complete Christian life. I confess that I often fall short. Forgive me for any hypocrisy and help me find gravitate for all the blessings in my life. I ask for the grace to grow in genuine love and faith, that I may be not just 'almost,' but 'completely' yours."

The Scripture Way of Salvation

May 22nd 1758

Introduction

At the time this sermon was first delivered the Methodist movement was in the midst of a time of rapid growth. Yet, with this rapid growth came the challenge of translating fervent faith into tangible, everyday living. John Wesley, the movement's founder, recognized this crucial need. He understood that the core of Christianity, while profound, could be obscured by complex theological jargon, leaving many struggling to grasp its practical application. In this sermon, Wesley cuts through the theological fog, offering clear and accessible guidance on the very heart of salvation and faith, drawing directly from Ephesians 2:8. He delves into the fundamental questions of what it means to be saved, what constitutes saving faith, and how that faith empowers us to live a life transformed by God's grace, providing practical wisdom for a movement needing direction.

Summary

In this sermon John Wesley argues that true Christian salvation, as presented in the Bible, is simple: the goal is salvation, and the way to achieve it is faith. It emphasizes the importance of understanding these two key concepts accurately. Salvation is not just a future reward in heaven but a present reality, encompassing God's work in us from initial grace to ultimate glory. This includes justification (pardon for sins) and sanctification (becoming more Christ-like). The text acknowledges the ongoing struggle with sin even after justification, emphasizing the need for continual repentance and growth in grace.

Wesley defines faith as a divinely given conviction of unseen realities, specifically the belief that Christ loved me and died for me. This faith leads to receiving Christ and trusting in God. Crucially, the author argues that faith is the sole condition for both justification and sanctification. While repentance and good works are important, they are necessary for faith, not instead of faith. Wesley advocates for expecting full sanctification – complete freedom from sin through perfect love – as a present possibility received through faith, urging believers to expect this transformative work of God in their lives now.

Modernized text

For by grace you have been saved through faith, and this is not your own doing; it is the gift of God - Ephesians 2:8

1. Religion, as it's often presented, can be incredibly complicated and difficult to understand. This is true not only of pagan religions, even those of the most intelligent pagans, but also of the religions of some who call themselves Christians, even famous and influential Christians. However, the true religion of Jesus Christ is simple and easy to understand if we take it just as it's presented in the Bible. The wise Creator and Governor of the world designed it perfectly to fit the limited understanding and capacity of humans in our present condition. This is evident both in the goal it sets before us and the way to reach that goal. The goal, simply put, is salvation; the way to achieve it is faith.

2. It's clear that these two small words—faith and salvation—contain the essence of the entire Bible, the core of all Scripture. Therefore, we should be absolutely certain we understand them correctly and accurately.

3. So let's seriously consider these questions:

I. What is salvation?
II. What is the faith that saves us?
III. How does faith save us?

What is Salvation?

1. First, let's ask, "What is salvation?" The salvation being discussed here isn't simply going to heaven or experiencing eternal happiness after death. It's not about

the soul entering paradise, what Jesus called "Abraham's bosom." It's not a blessing that awaits us in the afterlife. The text itself makes this clear: "You are saved." Salvation isn't something distant; it's a present reality, a blessing you possess right now through God's free mercy. In fact, the words could also be translated as "You have been saved," meaning that salvation encompasses God's entire work in us, from the first glimmer of grace in our souls until it reaches its fullness in glory.

2. Understood broadly, salvation includes everything God does in our souls through what's often called "natural conscience," but more accurately, "preventing grace"— God's initial pull toward Godself; the desires for God that grow stronger when we embrace them; the light of Christ that illuminates everyone, showing them how to live justly, love mercy, and walk humbly with God; and the convictions that the Holy Spirit stirs within each person— though most people suppress these convictions quickly, eventually forgetting, or even denying, that they ever felt them.

3. But our focus here is on the salvation the Apostle is specifically addressing. This salvation has two main aspects: justification and sanctification. Justification simply means pardon. It's the forgiveness of all our sins and our acceptance by God. The price paid to secure this for us (what's often called "the meritorious cause of our justification") is the blood and righteousness of Christ—or, more clearly, everything Christ did and suffered for us, culminating in his death for sinners. The immediate results of justification are the peace of God, a peace that

transcends understanding, and a joyful hope of God's glory, a joy beyond words and full of glory.

4. The moment we are justified, sanctification also begins. At that instant, we are born again, born from above, born of the Spirit. A genuine transformation occurs. We are inwardly renewed by God's power. We experience God's love flooding our hearts through the Holy Spirit, producing love for all people, especially fellow Christians. This love drives out our love for the world—love of pleasure, comfort, status, and wealth—along with pride, anger, selfishness, and all other harmful attitudes. In short, it transforms our worldly, self-centered, sinful nature into the mind of Christ.

5. It's natural for those who experience such a change to think that all sin is gone, completely uprooted from their hearts. They easily conclude, "I don't feel any sin, so I must not have any. It's not stirring, so it doesn't exist. It's not active, so it's not there."

6. But they soon discover that sin was only dormant, not eradicated. Temptations reappear, and sin resurfaces, proving it was merely suppressed, not eliminated. They now feel two opposing forces within themselves: their sinful nature warring against the Spirit of God. They can't deny that even though they still have the power to believe in Christ and love God, even though the Holy Spirit assures them they are God's children, they still experience pride, selfishness, anger, and doubt. They find these things stirring within them, though not always victorious. These temptations may even fiercely assault them, but the Lord helps them.

7. Macarius, writing fourteen centuries ago, accurately described the experience of believers: "Those lacking skill [or experience], when they feel God's grace, immediately imagine they no longer have sin. But those with discernment know that even those of us who experience God's grace can be troubled by sin again. We've often seen examples among fellow believers who experienced such grace that they claimed to be without sin. Yet later, when they thought themselves completely free from sin, the corruption hidden within them resurfaced, and they were nearly consumed by it."

8. From the moment of our new birth, the ongoing work of sanctification begins. The Holy Spirit empowers us to put to death the sinful deeds of our human nature. As we die more and more to sin, we become more and more alive to God. We grow in grace as we diligently avoid all evil and eagerly pursue good works whenever possible, doing good to everyone. We participate faithfully in spiritual practices, worshiping God in spirit and truth. We embrace self-denial, giving up any pleasure that doesn't draw us closer to God.

9. In this way, we anticipate complete sanctification, a full salvation from all our sins—pride, selfishness, anger, and unbelief—or, as the Apostle Paul says, we "press on toward perfection." But what is perfection? The word has various meanings; here it means perfect love. It is a love that leaves no room for sin, a love that fills our hearts completely. It is a love that rejoices always, prays constantly, and gives thanks in all circumstances.

II. What is Faith?

10. The Apostle Paul defines faith generally as "being sure of what we hope for and certain of what we do not see." It is a divine evidence and conviction of unseen realities—things not visible or perceivable through our physical senses. It involves a supernatural revelation of God and spiritual realities, a kind of spiritual light illuminating the soul, enabling us to see them. Scripture speaks of God sometimes giving the light itself and sometimes the ability to perceive it. As Paul writes, "For God, who said, 'Let light shine out of darkness,' made his light shine in our hearts to give us the light of the knowledge of God's glory displayed in the face of Christ." Elsewhere, Paul speaks of "the eyes of hearts being enlightened." Through this twofold work of the Holy Spirit, our spiritual eyes are opened and illuminated, allowing us to see what our physical senses cannot perceive. We glimpse the invisible things of God; we see the spiritual world around us, a world normally imperceptible to our natural senses. We also see the eternal world, piercing through the veil that separates time and eternity. The clouds and darkness that once obscured it are gone, and we begin to see the glory that will be revealed.

11. More specifically, faith is a divine assurance and conviction not only that "God was reconciling the world to himself in Christ," but also that Christ loved me and gave himself for me. Through this faith (whether we call it the essence of faith or one of its qualities), we receive Christ in all his roles—as our Prophet, Priest, and King. Through faith, Christ becomes for us wisdom from God, righteousness, sanctification, and redemption.

12. Some ask, "Is this the faith of assurance, or the faith of adherence?" Scripture makes no such distinction. The Apostle Paul says, "There is one faith, and one hope to which God has called you." There is one Christian, saving faith, "just as there is one Lord," in whom we believe, "and one God and Father of all." This faith necessarily includes an assurance (another word for evidence) that Christ loved me and gave himself for me. For "whoever believes" with true, living faith "has this testimony in himself": "The Spirit himself testifies with our spirit that we are God's children." "Because you are his sons, God sent the Spirit of his Son into our hearts, the Spirit who calls out, 'Abba, Father.'" This gives us assurance that we are God's children and a childlike trust in God. It's important to note that assurance naturally comes before confidence. We can't have childlike trust in God until we know we are God's children. Therefore, trust, confidence, reliance, or whatever we call it, isn't the first but the second aspect of faith.

13. This is the faith by which we are saved, justified, and sanctified, using "sanctified" in its fullest sense. But how are we justified and sanctified by faith? This is our next question, and a crucial one. Because of its importance, we'll examine it more closely.

III. How We Are Saved by Faith

14. First, how are we justified by faith? What does this mean? My answer is this: Faith is the condition, and the only condition, of justification. It's the condition because only those who believe are justified. No one is justified

without faith. And it's the only condition because it's sufficient for justification. Everyone who believes is justified, regardless of anything else. In other words, no one is justified until they believe, and everyone is justified the moment they believe.

15. Some object, "But doesn't God also command us to repent and to 'produce fruit in keeping with repentance'—to stop doing evil and learn to do good? Aren't both repentance and good works absolutely necessary, so much so that if we intentionally neglect them, we can't expect to be justified? If that's the case, how can you say that faith is the only condition for justification?" God certainly commands us to repent and produce the fruit of repentance. If we deliberately ignore these commands, we shouldn't expect to be justified. So, repentance and good works are necessary for justification in a sense. However, they aren't necessary in the same way or to the same degree as faith. They aren't necessary to the same degree because those fruits are only required if there's time and opportunity for them. Someone can be justified without them, as the criminal on the cross was (if we can even call him a criminal, since a recent writer claims he was an honest and respectable person!). But no one can be justified without faith; that's impossible. Even if someone experiences deep repentance and does many good deeds, it won't justify them until they believe. But the instant they believe, with or without those fruits, with more or less repentance, they are justified. Repentance and its fruits are not necessary in the same way as faith because they're only indirectly necessary—necessary for faith—while faith is directly

necessary for justification. Therefore, faith remains the only condition directly and immediately necessary for justification.

16. Some ask, "Do you believe we're sanctified by faith? We now you believe we're justified by faith, but don't you believe and teach that we're sanctified by our works?" This claim has been made loudly and forcefully for twenty-five years, but I have always maintained the opposite, stating clearly and repeatedly, both privately and publicly, that we are sanctified by faith just as we are justified by faith. Indeed, these two great truths illuminate each other. Just as faith is the sole condition for justification, so it is the sole condition for sanctification. Only those who believe are sanctified; no one is sanctified without faith. And faith alone is sufficient for sanctification. Everyone who believes is sanctified, regardless of anything else. In other words, no one is sanctified until they believe, and everyone is sanctified the moment they believe.

17. Some ask, "Isn't there a repentance after justification as well as a repentance before justification? And aren't those who are justified obligated to be 'zealous for good works'? Aren't these so essential that if someone deliberately neglects them, they can't expect to be fully sanctified—that is, perfected in love? Can they even grow in grace and in the knowledge and love of our Lord Jesus Christ? Can they maintain the grace they've received? Can they continue in faith and in God's favor? Don't you yourself acknowledge

and constantly affirm all of this? But if so, how can you claim that faith is the only condition for sanctification?"

18. I do acknowledge and affirm all of this as God's truth. I agree that there's a repentance that follows justification as well as a repentance that precedes it. It is the duty of all who are justified to be zealous for good works. These are so essential that if we deliberately neglect them, we can't expect to be sanctified; we can't grow in grace, in the likeness of God, in the mind of Christ. Indeed, we can't even maintain the grace we've already received. We can't continue in faith or in God's favor. What does this mean? It means that both repentance, properly understood, and the practice of good works—acts of devotion as well as acts of compassion (rightly called "good works" because they stem from faith)—are necessary for sanctification in some sense.

19. I say "repentance, properly understood" because this kind of repentance is different from the repentance that comes before justification. Repentance after justification doesn't involve guilt, condemnation, or a sense of God's wrath. It doesn't involve doubting God's favor or any "fear that has torment." This repentance is a conviction, produced by the Holy Spirit, of the sin that still lingers in our hearts; of the "carnal nature" that, as our Church teaches, remains even in those who are born again, though it no longer rules over them. It's a conviction of our tendency toward evil, our inclination to backslide, the ongoing struggle of our sinful nature against the Spirit. Unless we constantly watch and pray, this sinful nature tempts us toward pride, anger, love for the world, love of comfort, status, or pleasure more

than love for God. It tempts us toward selfishness, unbelief, and idolatry, constantly pulling us away from the living God in countless ways and under countless pretexts.

20. Along with this conviction of indwelling sin, we also clearly see the sin that remains in our lives, clinging to everything we say and do. Even in our best actions, we now recognize a mixture of imperfection, whether in our motives, the actions themselves, or the way we perform them—something that wouldn't stand up to God's righteous judgment if God were to strictly examine our faults. Where we least expect it, we find traces of pride, selfishness, unbelief, or idolatry. We become more ashamed of our best efforts than we once were of our worst sins. We realize that even our good deeds have no merit in themselves and could not withstand God's justice. We would be guilty even for these if it weren't for the blood of Christ's covenant.

21. Experience confirms that, along with this awareness of sin in our hearts and lives, and the guilt we would deserve if not for the continual cleansing of Christ's blood, this repentance also includes recognizing our utter helplessness. We are incapable of thinking a single good thought or forming a single good desire on our own, much less speaking a good word or performing a good deed, except through God's free and almighty grace, which first draws us to God and then empowers us every step of the way.

22. Some ask, "What are the good works you say are necessary for sanctification?" First, there are acts of devotion: public worship, family prayer, private prayer; receiving Holy Communion; studying the Scriptures

through hearing, reading, and meditation; and fasting or abstaining from certain things as our health permits.

23. Second, there are acts of compassion, whether meeting physical or spiritual needs: feeding the hungry, clothing the naked, welcoming strangers, visiting those in prison or who are sick or suffering; instructing the uninformed, awakening those lost in sin, encouraging those who are lukewarm in their faith, strengthening those who doubt, comforting the discouraged, helping those facing temptation, or contributing in any way to the salvation of others. This is the repentance, and these are the fruits of repentance, necessary for full sanctification. This is how God has instructed us to pursue complete salvation.

24. This shows the great harm caused by the seemingly harmless belief that believers no longer have sin, that all sin is completely eradicated the moment we are justified. By preventing this kind of repentance, it completely blocks the path to sanctification. There's no room for repentance in those who believe they have no sin in their hearts or lives. Consequently, there's no room for them to be perfected in love, for which this repentance is absolutely essential.

25. This also shows that there's no danger in expecting full salvation. Even if we were mistaken, even if such a blessing were unattainable, we would still lose nothing. In fact, this very expectation motivates us to use all the gifts God has given us, developing them fully so that when our Lord returns, he will receive what is his with increase.

26. To return to our main point: While this repentance and its fruits are necessary for full salvation, they aren't

necessary in the same way or to the same degree as faith. They aren't necessary to the same degree because these fruits are only conditionally necessary—if there is time and opportunity for them. Otherwise, someone can be sanctified without them. But no one can be sanctified without faith. Even if someone demonstrates deep repentance and does many good works, these alone won't sanctify them until they believe. But the moment they believe, with or without those fruits, with more or less repentance, they are sanctified. Repentance and its fruits are not necessary in the same way as faith because they're only indirectly necessary—necessary for the continuation and growth of faith—while faith is directly and immediately necessary for sanctification. Therefore, faith remains the only condition directly and immediately necessary for sanctification.

27. Some ask, "What kind of faith saves us from sin and perfects us in love?" First, it's a divine assurance and conviction that God has promised this in Scripture. Until we are fully convinced of this, we can't move forward. One would think no further proof would be needed than God's ancient promise: "I will circumcise your hearts and the hearts of your descendants, so that you may love the Lord your God with all your heart and with all your soul, and live." How clearly this speaks of being perfected in love! How strongly it implies being saved from all sin! When love completely fills our hearts, there's no room left for sin.

28. Second, it's a divine assurance and conviction that God is able to do what God has promised. Even if it's

"impossible for people" to make something clean from something unclean," to purify the heart from all sin and fill it with holiness, this poses no problem for God, because "with God all things are possible." Surely no one would imagine this possible for any power less than God's! But when God speaks, it is done. God said, "Let there be light," and there was light!

29. Third, it's a divine assurance and conviction that God is able and willing to do this now. And why not? Isn't a moment the same as a thousand years to God? God doesn't need more time to accomplish God's will. And God isn't waiting for us to become more worthy or deserving of God's favor. Therefore, we can confidently declare at any time, "Now is the day of salvation!" "Today, if you hear his voice, do not harden your hearts!" "See, I have prepared my dinner; my oxen and fattened cattle have been butchered, and everything is ready. Come to the wedding banquet."

30. To this confidence in God's ability and willingness to sanctify us now, one more thing must be added — a divine assurance and conviction that God is doing it. At that moment, it is done. God says to our innermost being, "According to your faith, let it be done to you!" Then the soul is cleansed from every stain of sin; it is purified from all unrighteousness. The believer then experiences the profound truth of these words: "But if we walk in the light, as he is in the light, we have fellowship with one another, and the blood of Jesus, his Son, purifies us from all sin."

31. Some ask, "Does God do this great work gradually or instantaneously?" It may be gradual for some, in the

sense that they don't realize the specific moment when sin ceases. But it's highly desirable, if it's God's will, for it to happen instantly, for the Lord to destroy sin "by the breath of his mouth" in a moment, in the twinkling of an eye. And this is often how God works—a plain fact with ample evidence to convince anyone open to the truth. So expect it at any moment! Expect it in the way described above, as you diligently pursue the good works for which you have been "created in Christ Jesus." There's no risk in this expectation. You won't be worse off if it doesn't happen immediately. Even if you were disappointed, you would lose nothing. But you won't be disappointed; it will come, and it won't be long. Expect it every day, every hour, every moment! Why not this very hour, this very moment? You can certainly expect it now if you believe it comes by faith. Here's how you can tell if you're seeking it by faith or by works: if by works, you think you must do something first before being sanctified—"I must first be or do this or that"—then you are still seeking it through your own efforts. But if you seek it by faith, expect it just as you are, and expect it now. Remember the vital connection between these three things: expect it by faith, expect it as you are, and expect it now! To deny one is to deny all; to affirm one is to affirm all. Do you believe we are sanctified by faith? Then live by this principle and expect this blessing just as you are, no better and no worse, as a sinner with nothing to offer but the fact that "Christ died." And if you expect it just as you are, expect it now. Don't wait for anything. Why should you? Christ is ready, and he is all you need. He's waiting for you; he's at the door! Let your heart cry out,

"Come in, come in, thou heavenly Guest!
Nor hence again remove;
But sup with me, and let the feast
Be everlasting love."

Key Points

- **Salvation is present**: Salvation isn't just about the afterlife; it's a present reality experienced now through God's grace. It encompasses both justification (forgiveness) and sanctification (becoming more like Christ).

- **Justification by faith alone:** We are justified (forgiven and accepted by God) through faith in Jesus Christ. Repentance and good works are important, but they are fruits of faith, not the basis of our justification.

- **Sanctification by faith alone:** Just as we are justified by faith, so too are we sanctified by faith. It is the same faith that justifies us that also empowers us to grow in holiness. Again, good works are a result of sanctification, not the cause.

- **Ongoing struggle with sin**: Even after justification, believers still experience the struggle with sin. Sanctification is a process, a gradual (and sometimes instantaneous) work of the Holy Spirit.

- **Faith as assurance and conviction:** Saving faith involves not only intellectual assent but also a deep, personal assurance that Christ loved me and gave himself for me. This assurance leads to childlike trust in God.

- **Sanctification is both gradual and instantaneous:** While sanctification is a process, Wesley emphasizes that it can also be an instantaneous experience. We should expect it by faith, expect it as we are, and expect it now. It is a gift freely offered and available to all who believe.

Personal Reflection Questions

- Do I truly believe that salvation is a present reality, available to me now? How does this belief impact my daily life and choices?
- Am I relying on my own efforts and good works to earn God's favor, or am I trusting solely in the grace offered through faith in Jesus Christ?
- Am I open to the possibility of sanctification? What steps can I take to cultivate a faith that expects and receives this blessing?

Prayer Prompts

Morning: "Lord Jesus, I thank you for the gift of salvation, both now and forever. Help me to live in the reality of your grace today, trusting in your forgiveness and allowing your Spirit to transform me from the inside out. May I experience the fullness of your love and walk in the power of your sanctifying presence."

Evening: "Father, I am grateful for your unwavering love and mercy. I confess that I still struggle with sin, even as I desire to follow you. I ask for the grace to repent where I have fallen short and the faith to believe in your power to cleanse and sanctify me. Thank you for the assurance that you are working in me, even when I don't see it. Help me to trust in your timing and expect your perfect work in my life."

AWAKENED WORDS

Catholic Spirit

Sept. 8th 1749

Introductions

England in the 18th century was a nation grappling with religious divisions. Tensions simmered between Protestants and Catholics, fueled by historical conflicts and lingering suspicions. Adding to this complex landscape, the Methodist movement, though still within the Church of England, was rapidly evolving. Distinct practices in worship and spiritual life were emerging, setting Methodists apart and raising questions about their future. While John Wesley, a staunch Anglican priest, did not envision a separate denomination, the growing number of "dissenting" congregations, independent Protestant churches outside the Church of England, offered a compelling alternative model. In this climate of shifting allegiances and burgeoning religious identity, Wesley addresses the critical issue of Christian unity, exploring the delicate balance between maintaining doctrinal conviction and extending the hand of fellowship to all believers. His sermon "Catholic Spirit" offers timely guidance for a movement at a crossroads, seeking to define its own identity while navigating the broader landscape of English Christianity.

Summery

John Wesley uses Jehu and Jehonadab's encounter in 2 Kings as a springboard to discuss Christian unity and a "catholic spirit." He argues that while love is owed to all, a special love exists for fellow believers. However, differing beliefs and worship practices often hinder this love. Wesley emphasizes that these differences shouldn't prevent unity of affection.

He focuses on Jehu's question, "Is your heart as true to mine as mine is to yours?" Wesley highlights that Jehu didn't inquire about Jehonadab's beliefs or worship style, despite their likely differences. Wesley argues that while individuals should hold their own beliefs sincerely, no one can be certain of the absolute truth of all their combined opinions. He stresses tolerance and allowing others freedom of conscience. He also acknowledges the diversity of worship practices even within Christianity, emphasizing that each person must follow their own conscience. He doesn't impose his own preferences but asks only: "Is your heart right with God, as my heart is with God?"

Wesley then explores what it means for a heart to be "right with God," questioning belief in God's attributes, faith in Christ, love for God and neighbor, dedication to God's will, fear of displeasing God, and active pursuit of good works. He emphasizes loving one's neighbor as oneself, including enemies. If these qualities are present, Wesley urges, "give me your hand," meaning: love me as a fellow Christian, pray for me, encourage me, and support me in God's work.

Finally, Wesley defines a "catholic spirit." It's not indifference to doctrine, worship, or congregation. Rather, it's a love that transcends these differences. A person with a catholic spirit is firmly committed to their own beliefs and practices, but simultaneously embraces all whose hearts are right with God, regardless of their opinions, worship style, or church affiliation. This catholic spirit manifests in constant care, prayer, advocacy, encouragement, and practical help for all believers. It is, at its core, universal love.

Modernized text

When he left there, he met Jehonadab son of Rechab coming to meet him; he greeted him, and said to him, 'Is your heart as true to mine as mine is to yours?' Jehonadab answered, 'It is.' Jehu said, 'If it is, give me your hand.' So he gave him his hand. Jehu took him up with him into the chariot. -2 Kings 10:15

1. Everyone acknowledges that we owe love to all people. The most important rule is, "Love your neighbor as yourself," which is clear to everyone. This isn't the limited version from past fanatics: "Love your neighbor—your family, friends, and acquaintances—and hate your enemy." No! Jesus said, "Love your enemies, bless those who curse you, do good to those who hate you, and pray for those who mistreat and persecute you, so that you may be children of your Father in heaven. He causes his sun to rise on good and bad people alike. He sends rain to those who do right and those who do wrong."

2. We certainly have a special love for those who love God. David said, "My delight is in the godly people of the land, the righteous who are honored." And someone greater than David said, "I give you a new command: Love each other. Just as I have loved you, you must love each other. By this everyone will know that you are my disciples, if you love each other" (John 13:34-35). The Apostle John emphasized this love: "This is the message you heard from the beginning: We should love each other" (1 John 3:11). "This is how we know what love is: Jesus Christ laid down his life for us. And we ought to lay down our lives for our

brothers and sisters" (1 John 3:16). And again: "Dear friends, let us love one another, for love comes from God. Everyone who loves has been born of God and knows God" (1 John 4:7-8). "This is love: not that we loved God, but that he loved us and sent his Son as an atoning sacrifice for our sins. Dear friends, since God so loved us, we also ought to love one another" (1 John 4:10-11).

3. Everyone agrees with this, but do they practice it? Experience says no. Where are the Christians who "love each other as he has commanded us?" So many things get in the way! The two main obstacles are: First, we can't all think the same. Second, because of this, we can't all act the same. Our actions differ in minor ways because our opinions differ.

4. But differing opinions or ways of worship don't have to stop us from loving each other. Can't we be united in affection, even if we disagree? Can't we be of one heart, even if we aren't of one mind? Absolutely! All of God's children can be united, even with these small differences. Instead of causing division, these differences can help us encourage each other in love and good deeds.

5. Every serious Christian should pay attention to and imitate the example of Jehu, despite his flaws. "Jehu left there and met Jehonadab son of Rechab, who was coming to meet him. Jehu greeted him and said, 'Are you as loyal to me as I am to you?' 'Yes, I am,' Jehonadab replied. 'If so,' said Jehu, 'give me your hand.'"

This passage has two parts: First, Jehu asks Jehonadab a question: "Are you as loyal to me as I am to you?" Second, Jehonadab answers, "Yes, I am," and Jehu offers him his hand: "If so, give me your hand."

Let's start by considering Jehu's question to Jehonadab: "Are you as loyal to me as I am to you?"

6. The first thing to notice is that Jehu doesn't ask about Jehonadab's beliefs. Jehonadab had very unusual beliefs, unique to himself. These beliefs strongly influenced his actions, and he insisted that his descendants follow them forever. We know this from Jeremiah's account years later: "Then I took Jaazaniah...his brothers and all his sons —the whole family of the Rechabites... I set bowls full of wine and some cups before them and said, 'Drink some wine!' But they replied, 'We will not drink wine, because Jonadab son of Rechab, our ancestor (Jehonadab was their ancestor), gave us this command: "Neither you nor your descendants must ever drink wine. Also, you must never build houses, sow seeds, plant vineyards, or own any of these things; you must live in tents all your lives...." We have obeyed everything our ancestor Jonadab commanded us'" (Jeremiah 35:3-10).

7. Jehu, known for his forceful personality in both secular and religious matters, doesn't worry about any of this. He lets Jehonadab have his own opinions. Neither man seems concerned with the other's differing beliefs.

8. Many good people today hold unique beliefs, some as unusual as Jehonadab's. As long as we only know in part, we won't all see things the same way. It's inevitable, given our limited understanding, that people will have different opinions about religion and life. It's been that way

since the beginning and will continue "until everything is restored."

9. While we must believe that each of our own opinions is true (because not believing it means we wouldn't hold it), no one can be certain that all of their opinions together are completely true. Every thoughtful person knows they are not. As the saying goes, "humanum est errare et nescire": "To be ignorant of many things and mistaken in some is part of being human." We know we are mistaken in some ways, even if we don't know exactly where.

10. We may not be able to know where we are wrong. Who can fully grasp how much invincible ignorance or deeply ingrained prejudice can affect our thinking? These things can be so deeply rooted that it's impossible to remove them. Unless we know every detail, who can judge how responsible someone is for a mistake? Guilt requires intent, and only God, who sees into the heart, can judge that.

11.Wise people let others think for themselves, just as they want to be allowed to think for themselves. They don't insist that others agree with them. They're tolerant of differences and ask only one thing of those they want to unite with in love: "Is your heart right with God, as my heart is with God?"

12. We also don't see Jehu asking about Jehonadab's style of worship, even though they likely differed greatly in this area. Jehonadab and his family probably worshiped God in Jerusalem, while Jehu did not, prioritizing political strategy over religious purity. Though he killed Baal's worshipers and got rid of Baal worship in

Israel, he continued the convenient sin of Jeroboam: worshiping golden calves (2 Kings 10:29).

13. Even sincere people who want to "keep a clear conscience" will have different ways of worshiping God because of their differing beliefs. Throughout history, people have disagreed about the nature of God and, even more, about how to worship God. It's not surprising in the outside world, because they "did not know God through their wisdom" and therefore didn't know how to worship God. But it's strange that even in the Christian world, where everyone agrees that "God is spirit, and his worshipers must worship in the Spirit and in truth," there are as many different ways of worshipping God as there were among the others.

14. How do we choose from so many options? No one can choose for or tell another person what to do. Each of us must follow our conscience with sincerity and devotion to God. We must be fully convinced in our own minds and then act according to what we believe is right. No one has the right to force others to follow their rules. God hasn't given anyone the authority to control the consciences of others. Each person must judge for themselves, because each person will answer to God.

15. Every follower of Christ is obligated by their faith to belong to a particular congregation or church, which implies a specific way of worship (since "can two walk together, except they be agreed?" Amos 3:3). However, no earthly power can force someone to prefer one congregation or form of worship over another, only their own conscience can do that. It's often thought that we should belong to the church of the place where we were

born. For example, someone born in England should belong to the Church of England and worship in its way. I used to strongly believe this, but I now have reasons to doubt it. It causes problems that no reasonable person can ignore, the biggest being that it would have prevented the Reformation, which depended on the right of individuals to judge for themselves.

16. I won't force my way of worship on anyone else. I believe it is truly based on the earliest Christian practices, but my belief isn't a rule for others. So, I don't ask those I want to unite with in love: "Are you a member of my church or congregation? Do you follow our form of church government and have the same church leaders? Do you worship with the same prayers I use?" I don't ask if you celebrate the Lord's Supper in the same way or if you agree with me about infant baptism, how it should be done, or who should receive it. I don't even ask if you believe in baptism and the Lord's Supper at all, as certain as I am about those things. Let's set those things aside for now. We can discuss them later if needed. My only question is this: "Is your heart right with God, as my heart is with God?"

17. To accurately represent the question, I do not mean, What did Jehu imply by his question but what would a follower of Christ imply if they repeated the question to any of their fellow believers.

The first question is this: Is your heart right with God? Do you believe in God's existence and perfections—God's eternity, immensity, wisdom, and power, God's justice, mercy, and truth? Do you believe that God now "sustains all things by his powerful word" (Hebrews 1:3), and that

God governs even the smallest and most harmful things for his glory and the good of those who love him? Do you have a divine assurance, a supernatural conviction, about the things of God? Do you "live by faith, not by sight" (2 Corinthians 5:7), focusing not on temporary things but on eternal ones?

18. Do you believe in the Lord Jesus Christ, "God over all, forever praised!" (Romans 9:5)? Has Christ been revealed in your soul? Do you know Jesus Christ and him crucified? Does Christ live in you, and you in him? Is Christ formed in your heart through faith? Having completely renounced your own works and righteousness, have you "submitted yourselves to the righteousness of God, which comes through faith in Jesus Christ" (Romans 3:22)? Are you "found in him, not having a righteousness of your own that comes from the law, but that which is through faith in Christ" (Philippians 3:9)? And through him, are you "fighting the good fight of the faith, taking hold of the eternal life" (1 Timothy 6:12)?

19. Is your faith *energoumenh di agaphs*—filled with the power of love? Do you love God (I don't say "above all things," because that phrase isn't in Scripture and is unclear), but "with all your heart and with all your soul and with all your mind and with all your strength" (Mark 12:30)? Do you seek all your happiness in God alone? And do you find what you seek? Does your soul continually "magnify the Lord, and your spirit rejoice in God your Savior" (Luke 1:46-47)? Having learned "to give thanks in all circumstances" (1 Thessalonians 5:18), do you find it "a joyful and pleasant thing to be thankful"? Is God the center of your soul, the sum of all your desires? Are you

therefore storing up your treasure in heaven and considering everything else as worthless (Matthew 6:20, Philippians 3:8)? Has the love of God cast the love of the world out of your soul? Then you are "crucified to the world" (Galatians 6:14); you are dead to everything below, and your "life is now hidden with Christ in God" (Colossians 3:3).

20. Are you employed in doing "not your own will, but the will of him who sent you" (John 5:30; 6:38)—of God who sent you down to live here awhile, to spend a few days in a foreign land, until, having finished the work God has given you to do, you return to your Father's house? Is it your food and drink "to do the will of your Father in heaven" (Matthew 6:10)? Is your eye single in all things, always fixed on him, always looking to Jesus? Do you point to him in everything you do, in all your work, your business, your conversation, aiming only at God's glory in everything, "whatever you do, whether in word or deed, do it all in the name of the Lord Jesus, giving thanks to God the Father through him" (Colossians 3:17)?

21. Does God's love compel you to serve him with fear, to "rejoice unto him with reverence" (Psalm 2:11)? Are you more afraid of displeasing God than you are of death or hell? Is nothing so terrible to you as the thought of offending his glorious presence? Because of this, do you "hate all evil ways" (Psalm 119:104), every transgression of his holy and perfect law, and therefore "strive to have a clear conscience before God and man" (Acts 24:16)?

22. Is your heart right toward your neighbor? Do you love all people, without exception, as yourself? "If you love those who love you, what reward will you get?" (Matthew

5:46). Do you "love your enemies" (Matthew 5:44)? Is your soul full of goodwill and tender affection towards them? Do you love even the enemies of God, the unthankful and unholy? Does your heart ache for them? Could you "wish that you yourself were cursed and cut off from Christ" for their sake (Romans 9:3)? And do you show this by "blessing those who curse you, praying for those who mistreat you" (Luke 6:28), and persecuting you?

23. Do you show your love by your actions? While you have time and opportunity, do you actually "do good to all people" (Galatians 6:10), neighbors or strangers, friends or enemies, good or bad? Do you do them all the good you can, trying to meet all their needs, helping them both physically and spiritually to the best of your ability? If you are like this, may every Christian say—if you sincerely desire this and are striving to reach it—then "your heart is right, as my heart is with your heart."

24. "If it is, give me your hand." I don't mean, "Agree with my opinions." You don't have to. I don't expect or want you to. Nor do I mean, "I will agree with your opinions." I can't; it doesn't depend on my choice. I can't think any more than I can see or hear as I will. Keep your opinions, and I'll keep mine, as firmly as ever. You don't even have to try to change my mind or me to change yours. I don't want you to argue about these points or to hear or say a word about them. Let's leave all opinions aside. Just "give me your hand."

25. I don't mean, "Embrace my forms of worship," or "I will embrace yours." This also doesn't depend on your choice or mine. We must each act according to what we are fully convinced of in our own minds. Hold firmly to

what you believe is most pleasing to God, and I will do the same. I believe the Episcopal form of church government is scriptural and based on early Christian practices. If you think the Presbyterian or Independent form is better, continue to think that and act accordingly. I believe infants should be baptized and that this can be done by immersion or sprinkling. If you believe differently, stay with your beliefs and follow your own convictions. I think forms of prayer are very useful, especially in large gatherings. If you think spontaneous prayer is more useful, act according to your own judgment. I believe I shouldn't withhold water from those who can be baptized and that I should eat bread and drink wine as a reminder of my dying Lord. But if you're not convinced of this, act according to your own understanding. I don't want to argue with you about any of these things. Let's set these minor points aside and never mention them. If your heart is like mine—if you love God and all people—I ask no more. Just "give me your hand."

26. I mean, first, love me. And not just as you love everyone, or even your enemies—those who hate you, "mistreat you, and persecute you" (Matthew 5:44); not just as you love a stranger, someone you know nothing good or bad about. I'm not satisfied with that. No, "if your heart is right, as my heart is with God," then love me with a very tender affection, as a friend who is closer than a brother (Proverbs 18:24); as a fellow Christian, a fellow citizen of the New Jerusalem, a fellow soldier engaged in the same battle under the same Captain, our Savior. Love me as a companion in the kingdom and patience of Jesus and a fellow heir of his glory.

27. Love me—even more than you love most people—with the love that is patient and kind. Be patient if I'm ignorant or wrong, supporting me instead of adding to my burden. Be tender, gentle, and compassionate. Don't be envious if God blesses my work more than yours. Love me with a love that isn't easily angered by my foolishness or weaknesses, or even if I seem to be acting against God's will. Love me in a way that assumes the best, putting aside all suspicion and negativity. Love me with a love that protects everything, never revealing my faults or weaknesses. Believe the best about me, always interpreting my words and actions in the most favorable light. Hope for the best—that whatever was said never happened, or didn't happen the way it was reported, or at least that it was done with good intentions or under pressure. And always hope that whatever is wrong will be corrected by God's grace, and whatever is lacking will be supplied through his rich mercy in Christ Jesus.

28. I also mean, pray for me constantly. Wrestle with God on my behalf, asking that God will quickly correct what God sees is wrong and provide what I lack. When you are closest to God, ask God, who is always present with you, that my heart may be more like yours, more right toward God and toward others; that I may have a fuller conviction of unseen realities and a stronger vision of God's love in Christ Jesus; that I may walk more steadily by faith, not by sight, and more earnestly grasp eternal life. Pray that the love of God and all people may be poured out into my heart more fully; that I may be more fervent and active in doing the will of our Father in heaven, more

zealous for good works, and more careful to avoid every appearance of evil.

29. I also mean, inspire me toward love and good deeds. Follow up your prayers by speaking to me in love whenever you believe it will benefit my soul. Encourage me in the work God has given me to do, and teach me how to do it more perfectly. Even "strike me in a friendly way and rebuke me" (Psalm 141:5) whenever you see me doing my own will instead of the will of God who sent me. Speak freely, whatever you think might correct my faults, strengthen my weaknesses, build me up in love, or make me more fit for the Master's service.

30. Finally, I mean love me not just with words, but with actions and truth. As far as your conscience allows (while still holding to your own beliefs and your way of worshiping God), join with me in God's work, and let's work together. You can certainly do this: Speak well of God's work and God's messengers, whoever they may be. And if you can, not only sympathize with them when they are in difficulty or distress, but give them cheerful and effective help so that they may glorify God.

31. Keep in mind two things about what I've said: First, whatever love, acts of love, or spiritual or practical help I ask from someone whose heart is right with God as mine is, I am ready, by God's grace, to give them the same, as best I can. Second, I'm not making this request just for myself, but for everyone whose heart is right toward God and others, so that we may all love one another as Christ has loved us.

32. We can draw one conclusion from what has been said: We can learn what a catholic spirit really is.

Few phrases have been more misunderstood and dangerously misused than this one. But anyone who carefully considers what I've said can easily correct these misunderstandings and prevent misuse.

From this, we can learn, first, that a catholic spirit isn't broad-mindedness about doctrine. It's not being indifferent to all opinions. That comes from hell, not from heaven. This instability of thought, this being "blown here and there by every wind of teaching" (Ephesians 4:14), is a curse, not a blessing, an irreconcilable enemy, not a friend, to true catholicism. Someone with a truly catholic spirit isn't still searching for their religion. They are firmly convinced of the core Christian doctrines. They are always willing to listen to and consider arguments against their beliefs, but this doesn't make them waver or blend different opinions. Be warned, you who don't know what spirit you have, you who call yourselves catholic simply because you are confused, because your mind is foggy, because you have no settled, consistent beliefs but just mix everything together. Realize you are lost and don't know where you are. You think you have Christ's spirit, but you're closer to the spirit of the Antichrist. First, learn the basic truths of the gospel, and then you will learn to have a truly catholic spirit.

33. We can learn, second, that a catholic spirit isn't broad-mindedness in practice. It's not indifference to public worship or the way it's done. That, too, would be a curse, not a blessing. It would hinder worshiping God in spirit and in truth. Someone with a truly catholic spirit has

carefully considered everything and has no doubt about the specific way they worship. They are fully convinced that this way of worship is scriptural and reasonable. They know of no other way that is more scriptural or reasonable. Therefore, they stick to it closely and praise God for the opportunity.

34. We can learn, third, that a catholic spirit isn't indifference to all congregations. This is another kind of broad-mindedness that is just as absurd and unscriptural as the others. It's far from the spirit of a truly catholic person. They are committed to their congregation as well as to their beliefs. They are united not only in spirit but also by the outward ties of Christian fellowship. There, they participate in all of God's ordinances. There, they receive the Lord's Supper. There, they pour out their soul in public prayer and join in praise and thanksgiving. There, they rejoice to hear the word of reconciliation, the gospel of God's grace. With their closest brothers and sisters, they seek God through fasting on special occasions. They watch over these people in love, as they do over their souls, encouraging, comforting, correcting, and building each other up in faith. They see these people as their own family and naturally care for them and ensure they have everything they need for life and godliness.

35. While they are firmly committed to their religious beliefs—to what they believe is the truth as it is in Jesus—while they firmly adhere to the way of worship that they believe is most pleasing to God, and while they are closely united to one particular congregation, their heart is open to all people, those they know and those they don't. They

embrace neighbors and strangers, friends and enemies, with strong and sincere affection. This is catholic or universal love, and those who have this love have a catholic spirit. Love alone earns this title: catholic love is a catholic spirit.

36. Therefore, in the fullest sense, someone with a catholic spirit is someone who, as I've described, welcomes all whose hearts are right with God. It's someone who appreciates and praises God for all the blessings they enjoy: their knowledge of God, the scriptural way of worshiping him, and especially their connection with a congregation that fears God and does what is right. While carefully guarding these blessings, keeping them close to their heart, they also love—as friends, as fellow Christians, as members of Christ and children of God, as fellow partakers of God's present kingdom, and as fellow heirs of his eternal kingdom—all who believe in the Lord Jesus Christ, who love God and others, who strive to please God and avoid offending him, and who are careful to avoid evil and eager to do good, regardless of their opinions, way of worship, or congregation. Someone with a truly catholic spirit constantly cares for all these people, feeling deep tenderness for them and longing for their well-being. They never stop praying for them and advocating for them. They encourage them and try to strengthen them in God through their words. They help them in every way they can, both spiritually and practically. They are ready to give everything for them, even their own lives.

Key Points

- *Love for all, special love for believers:* While we should love everyone, a special, deeper love exists for fellow Christians.

- *Unity despite differences:* Disagreements in belief or worship style shouldn't prevent Christians from loving one another. We can be united in affection even if we aren't of one mind.

- *Focus on the heart:* The most important question is not about specific beliefs or worship practices, but whether someone's heart is right with God. This involves genuine faith in Christ, love for God and neighbor, and a desire to do God's will.

- *"Giving your hand"*: This signifies a commitment to loving fellow Christians through tender affection, prayer, encouragement, and practical support.

- *Defining a "catholic spirit":* A truly catholic spirit isn't indifference to doctrine, worship, or church affiliation. It's about holding firm to one's own convictions while simultaneously loving and embracing all whose hearts are right with God, regardless of their differences.

- *Action-oriented love:* Love isn't just a feeling; it's expressed through concrete actions like prayer, encouragement, practical help, and speaking well of other believers.

Personal Reflection Questions

- Do I truly love my fellow Christians, even those with whom I disagree on points of doctrine or practice? How can I better express this love in concrete ways?
- Am I more focused on outward conformity or inward transformation? Do I prioritize having a heart right with God above insisting on agreement with all my opinions?
- In what specific ways can I cultivate a more "catholic spirit," embracing and supporting fellow believers who are different from me?

Prayer Prompts

Morning: "Lord, as I go into this day, help me to love my fellow Christians as you love them. May I be patient and kind, offering encouragement and support to those I encounter, even if we have different viewpoints. Show me how to 'give my hand' in practical ways, demonstrating your love through my actions."

Evening: "Thank you, Lord, for the fellowship of believers. I am grateful for those who have challenged and encouraged me today. Forgive me for any judgments I have made based on outward appearances or minor disagreements. Help me to cultivate a heart of love and acceptance, reflecting your catholic spirit."

JEREMY W SCOTT

Small Group Leader's Guide

This guide is designed to equip you to lead a small group study based on Awakened Words. Wesley's works offer a rich tapestry of theological insight, practical advice, and social commentary, providing fertile ground for discussion and spiritual growth. Remember, your role is to facilitate, not dictate. Create a safe and welcoming environment where everyone feels comfortable sharing their thoughts and perspectives.

Core Principles

- **Grace-filled Space:** Foster an atmosphere of acceptance and grace, where vulnerability and honest questions are encouraged.
- **Shared Leadership:** Encourage participation from all group members. Consider rotating roles like prayer leader, snack provider, or discussion facilitator.
- **Focus on Application:** The goal is not just to understand Wesley's words, but to apply them to our lives today.
- **Respectful Dialogue:** Encourage open discussion while maintaining respect for differing viewpoints. Avoid debating and focus on understanding.
- **Prayerful Dependence:** Begin and end each session with prayer, acknowledging our dependence on God's guidance.

Suggested Meeting Outline

Gathering & Opening Prayer (5-10 minutes)
- Welcome participants and create a relaxed atmosphere.
- Begin with a brief prayer, asking for God's presence and guidance in your discussion.

Reading & Reflection (30-45 minutes)
- *Shared Reading:* Read the selected passage(s) aloud together. This allows everyone to hear the text and follow along. Consider having different people read each week.
- *Initial Reactions:* Ask a simple opening question like, "What stood out to you in this passage?" or "What is your initial reaction to what Wesley is saying?"
- *Contextualizing Wesley:* Guide the group to consider the historical and social context of Wesley's writing. Ask questions like:
  - "What do you think was happening in Wesley's time that prompted him to write this?"
  - "What were some of the challenges and opportunities facing the church and society in the 18th century?"
  - "How might these circumstances have shaped Wesley's perspective?"
- *Applying to Today:* Bridge the gap between Wesley's time and our own. Ask questions like:
  - "Where do you see parallels between the issues Wesley addressed and the challenges we face today?"

- "How might Wesley's insights inform our understanding of [specific issue]?"
- "What practical steps can we take to apply Wesley's teachings to our lives, our families, and our communities?"
- **Personal Reflection:** Encourage personal reflection by asking:
  - "How does this passage speak to your own life and experiences?"
  - "What is God inviting you to learn or do through this passage?"
  - "What questions or struggles do you have in light of this reading?"

Sharing & Discussion (20-30 minutes)

(See Discussion Questions Guide)

Encourage open sharing based on the reflection questions. Remind participants to listen respectfully and avoid interrupting. Gently guide the conversation back to the text if it drifts too far afield. Offer your own insights and reflections, but prioritize creating space for others to share.

Closing Prayer & Next Steps (5-10 minutes)

- Summarize key takeaways from the discussion.
- Encourage participants to continue reflecting on the passage throughout the week.
- Assign reading for the next session (if applicable).
- Close with a prayer, thanking God for the insights gained and asking for guidance in applying them to daily life.

Discussion Question Guide

Preview the paragraphs you intent to cover that week. Create 3-4 group discussion questions that speak to wider topics you feel are raised in the reading. This can be on a contemporary issue or a wider topic that John Wesley routinely addresses. See the examples below.

Issue or Event: "Today we have seen several examples of [issue, injustice, challenge]. How does Wesley's advice from the past feel relevant to to this issue/event?"

On Grace: "Wesley emphasizes the importance of God's grace. How do you understand grace? How have you experienced it in your life?"

On Personal Holiness: "Wesley emphasized personal holiness. What does it mean to you to live a holy life? How does Wesley's understanding of holiness challenge or inspire you?"

Remember: This is a guide, not a rigid script. Be flexible and adapt the outline and questions to fit the specific needs and interests of your group. Most importantly, trust in the power of God's Word and the wisdom of John Wesley to transform lives.

Online Groups

As an alternative to doing in-person or hybrid small groups at a specific time you can create an opportunity for people to read along together and discuss electronically. This could look like a weekly email to participants with that weeks reading assignment along with a personal reflection question and a discussion question. Participants would then be encouraged to reply-all to the email with their responses. Alternatively, consider using a discussion platform like a Facebook Group, Discord, or similar space. You can post reading assignments and discussion questions an encourage replies.

These types of groups can be successful but require a different kind of attention by the facilitator. You will need to be the primary commenter, especially in the beginning, and do what you can to keep the conversation going. You may consider recording short videos of yourself offering your own personal insights from the reading in the initial post.

Printed in Great Britain
by Amazon

59345930R00059